Getting What You Want In A Negotiation By Learning How To Signal

How To Develop The Skill Of Effective Signaling In A Negotiation In Order To Get The Best Possible Outcome

"Practical, proven techniques that will help you get the best deal possible out of your next negotiation"

Dr. Jim Anderson

Published by:
Blue Elephant Consulting
Tampa, Florida

Copyright © 2017 by Dr. Jim Anderson

All rights reserved. No part of this book may be reproduced of transmitted in any form or by any means, electronic or mechanical, including photocopying, recording or by any information storage and retrieval system without written permission of the publisher, except for inclusion of brief quotations in a review.

Printed in the United States of America

Library of Congress Control Number: 2017900187

ISBN-13: 978-1542369534

ISBN-10: 1542369533

Warning – Disclaimer

The purpose of this book is to educate and entertain. This book does not promise or guarantee that anyone following the ideas, tips, suggestions, techniques or strategies will be successful. The author, publisher and distributor(s) shall have neither liability nor responsibility to anyone with respect to any loss or damage caused, or alleged to be caused, directly or indirectly by the information contained in this book.

Recent Books By The Author

Product Management

- Managing Your Product Manager Career: How Product Managers Can Find And Succeed In The Right Job

- How Product Managers Can Sell More Of Their Product: Tips & Techniques For Product Managers To Better Understand How To Sell Their Product

Public Speaking

- How To Organize A Speech In Order To Make Your Point: How to put together a speech that will capture and hold your audience's attention

- Changing How You Speak To Overcome Your Fear Of Speaking: Change techniques that will transform a speech into a memorable event

CIO Skills

- New IT Technology Issues Facing CIOs: How CIOs Can Stay On Top Of The Changes In The Technology That Powers The Company

- Keeping The Barbarians Out: How CIOs Can Secure Their Department and Company: Tips And Techniques For CIOs To Use In Order To Secure Both Their IT Department And Their Company

IT Manager Skills

- How IT Managers Can Use New Technology To Meet Today's IT Challenges: Technologies That IT Managers Can Use In Order to Make Their Teams More Productive

- How To Build High Performance IT Teams: Tips And Techniques That IT Managers Can Use In Order To Develop Productive Teams

Negotiating

- Exploring How To Get The Deal That You Want In A Negotiation: How To Develop The Skill Of Exploring What Is Possible In A Negotiation In Order To Reach The Best Possible Deal

- Use The Power Of Arguing To Win Your Next Negotiation: How To Develop The Skill Of Effective Arguing In A Negotiation In Order To Get The Best Possible Outcome

Miscellaneous

- How To Heal A Broken Leg – Fast!: Understanding how to deal with a broken leg in order to start walking again quickly

- How Software Defined Networking (SDN) Is Going To Change Your World Forever: The Revolution In Network Design And How It Affects

Note: See a complete list of books by Dr. Jim Anderson at the back of this book.

Acknowledgements

Any book like this one is the result of years of real-world work experience. In my over 25 years of working for 7 different firms, I have met countless fantastic people and I've been mentored by some truly exceptional ones. Although I've probably forgotten some of the people who made me the person that I am today, here is my attempt to finally give them the recognition that they so truly deserve:

- Thomas P. Anderson
- Art Puett
- Bobbi Marshall
- Bob Boggs

Dr. Jim Anderson

This book is dedicated to my wife Lori. None of this would have been possible without her love and support.

Thanks for the best 21 years of my life (so far)...!

Table Of Contents

SIGNALING IS THE KEY TO GETTING WHAT YOU WANT 9

ABOUT THE AUTHOR 11

CHAPTER 1: DEMANDS & DEADLINES: YOUR TWO BEST FRIENDS ... 16

CHAPTER 2: HOW TO DEAL WITH HARD CORE OPPOSITION 18

CHAPTER 3: DEATH TO DEADLINES! (OURS NOT THEIRS) 21

CHAPTER 4: REAL WORLD NEGOTIATING: BOEING VS. THE IAM 24

CHAPTER 5: HOW TO MAKE "TOTAL COST" WORK FOR YOU WHEN NEGOTIATING A SALE 27

CHAPTER 6: WHATEVER HAPPENED TO THAT BOEING NEGOTIATION? 31

CHAPTER 7: SAY HELLO TO THE BOGEY-MAN – A NEGOTIATOR'S BEST FRIEND 34

CHAPTER 8: NEGOTIATION AWARDS: WHO'S THE BEST NEGOTIATOR IN THE WORLD? 37

CHAPTER 9: IT'S NEGOTIATION TIME AT BOEING: PLANE & SIMPLE .41

CHAPTER 10: TOP 10 SECRETS TO MAKE A NEGOTIATION WORK OUT FOR YOU! 46

CHAPTER 11: NEGOTIATION FIRESTARTER: THE TAKE IT OR LEAVE IT TACTIC 50

CHAPTER 12: NEGOTIATING SELF DEFENSE: COUNTERING THE REVERSE AUCTION TACTIC 54

Signaling Is The Key To Getting What You Want

When we sit down to negotiate, we are really entering into a very specialized conversation with the other side of the table. We have a set of goals and they have their own set of goals. The purpose of the negotiation conversation is to find out if there is a way that the needs of both sides of the table can be met.

In order to find ways to move the negotiation forward, the other side is going to have to understand what we are trying to accomplish. They are going to have to know when something is important to us and when we really don't care about something. It is our obligation to communicate our intentions to the other side.

The way that we communicate what we want is by signaling to them. Signals are rarely spoken words. Instead, we need to find other ways to get our point across and let the other side know what we want them to do. This requires them to take the time to study us and to get to know us well enough to be able to pick up on our signals.

During a negotiation, signals can come in many different forms. One of the more common ones is a deadline. We may present the other side with a deadline in order to motivate them or they may present us with one. If we are facing a deadline, then we need to know how best to react to it in order to still be able to reach our negotiating goals.

A great way to become better at using signaling is to take the time to see how others use signaling in their negotiations. The classic example is in labor negotiations where both sides are using the press to attempt to communicate to the other side what they want them to do. In the past few years, Boeing has been involved in a number of negotiations and has done a very good job of signaling to the other side what the next steps need to be.

For more information on what it takes to be a great negotiator, check out my blog, The Accidental Negotiator, at:

www.TheAccidentalNegotiator.com

Good luck!

- Dr. Jim Anderson

About The Author

I must confess that I never set out to be a negotiator. When I went to school, I studied Computer Science and thought that I'd get a nice job programming and that would be that. Well, at least part of that plan worked out!

My first job was working for Boeing on their F/A-18 fighter jet program. I spent my days programming fighter jet software in assembly language and I loved it. The U.S. government decided to save some money and went looking for other countries to sell this plane to. This put me into an unfamiliar role: I started to negotiate with foreign military officials and I ended up having to participate in the negotiations for large international deals.

Time moved on and so did I. I found myself working for Siemens, the big German telecommunications company. They were making phone switches and selling them to the seven U.S. phone companies. The problem was that the switches were too complicated. When it came time to negotiate a deal with the customer, the sales teams struggled to create an effective negotiating strategy. I was called in to bridge the world between the product functionality and the business impacts as they related to the negotiations.

I've spent over 25 years working as a negotiator for both big companies and startups. This has given me an opportunity to learn what it takes to both plan and execute negotiations of all sizes. When it comes to negotiations, I've pretty much been there, done that.

I now live in Tampa Florida where I spend my time managing my consulting business, Blue Elephant Consulting, teaching college courses at the University of South Florida, and traveling to work with companies like yours to share the knowledge that I have about how to prepare for and execute successful negotiations.

I'm always available to answer questions and I can be reached at:

Dr. Jim Anderson
Blue Elephant Consulting
Email: jim@BlueElephantConsulting.com
Facebook: http://goo.gl/1TVoK
Web: **www.BlueElephantConsulting.com**

"Unforgettable communication skills that will set your ideas free..."

Create An Effective Negotiating Team At Your Company!

Dr. Jim Anderson is available to provide training and coaching on the topics that are the most important to people who have to negotiate: how can my team effectively prepare for and execute a successful negotiation that will get us what we both want and need?

Dr. Anderson believes that in order to both learn and remember what he says, audiences need to laugh. Each one of his speeches is full of fun and humor so that what he says "sticks" with everyone.

Dr. Anderson's Negotiating Training Includes:

1. How to plan for a negotiation: what information do you need and where can you find it?

2. What's the best way to explore how a deal can be created during a negotiation?

3. How can you bring a negotiation to a close without giving in to the other side?

Dr. Jim Anderson works with over 100 customers per year. To invite Dr. Anderson to work with you, contact him at:

Phone: 813-418-6970 or
Email: jim@BlueElephantConsulting.com

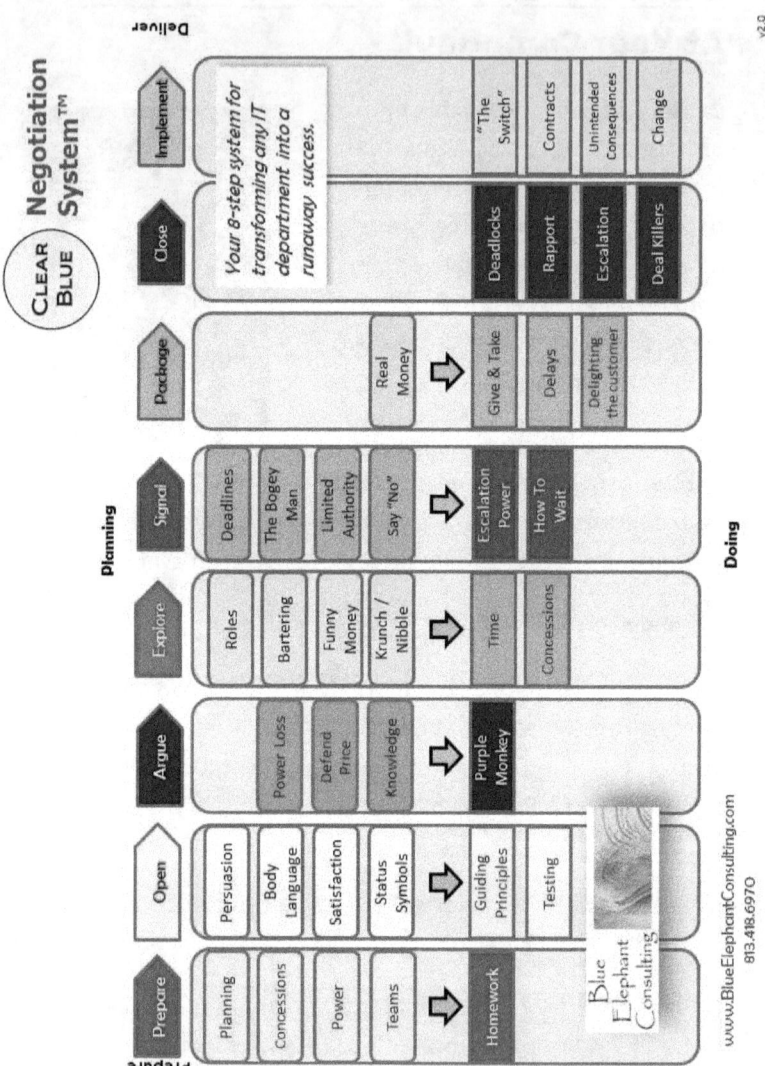

The **Clear Blue Negotiation System™** has been created to provide negotiators with a clear roadmap for how to manage a successful negotiation. This system shows negotiators what needs to be done and in what order to do it.

Chapter 1

Demands & Deadlines: Your Two Best Friends

Chapter 1: Demands & Deadlines: Your Two Best Friends

All too often when we are negotiating both in real life and in business, demands and deadlines show up. Since most of us have never been trained on how to deal with these issues, we tend to do the easiest thing: panic. May I suggest a different approach: ignore them.

Unless you are actively involved in a hostage negotiation, you probably won't be handed a list of demands. Instead, they will show up in more subtle ways. Casual statements like "This is a must have" or "I really don't have any flexibility on this issue" are the nice way of saying "this is a demand" in polite company.

Instead of panicking, great each veiled demand as an old friend. The other side has just revealed a point that is important to them. The actual demand does not matter that much, what really matters is the reason for the demand. If they say they need the delivery by Friday, then forget the demand and focus on why they need the delivery by then. Who is waiting for the delivery? Why do they need it then? Every demand is a step in the right direction because you now have a better idea about what key points the eventual solution must address.

Same thing goes for deadlines. If the other side says "we've got to wrap this up by 10 pm or we'll have to walk" then the question is why? What is their best alternative? What is so special about 10 pm? Why not continue tomorrow? Remember that most deadlines are garbage and the other side may be using them as part of a fairly poor attempt at moving the deal to a close. Ignore the deadline and move on. If they are interested in doing a deal, they'll end up ignoring it also.

Chapter 2

How To Deal With Hard Core Opposition

Chapter 2: How To Deal With Hard Core Opposition

We've talked about how to properly prepare to start a negotiation. Once we start to negotiate, thanks to millions of years of evolution, we are all pretty good at recognizing situations in which we are called on to compete. We are tuned to allow us to make ourselves heard in these situations and to get our point across. Which is why we all seem to do such a poor job when we are faced with no competition, but rather opposition. Oh, oh. What to do now?

So what is opposition? Opposition is what happens when the group of people that you are trying to communicate with are just dead set against what you have to say. If you show up in a situation where you are going to be telling your team about a great new documentation system that the company has mandated that everyone will start using, you will encounter opposition if nobody that you are talking to wants to do documentation in the first place — it's not that the new system is a bad idea (although it might be), it's just that everyone rejects the idea of doing documentation.

What's funny is that although in technical fields we struggle with how to deal with opposition, the folks who work in politics deal with it on a daily basis. Our elected officials are forced to deal with opposition every day and so they have developed effective ways of dealing with it. We could learn a thing or two from them:

Co-opt The Other Side's Issue: this is one of my favorite approaches. Don't go head-to-head with the opposition. Instead take a careful look at what's motivating their position: why doesn't your team want to do documentation? If you show respect for their underlying issue and then go ahead and propose a different way of solving it, you'll basically cut off the opposition at the knees. In our documentation case, if you show the team that offshore developers do a poor job of native language documentation and by doing a good job of documentation their work they will be able to keep more jobs onshore, then you've accomplished your co-opting.

Redefine The Issue: Initially an issue may start out as a tug-of-war. In order to solve this problem, if you redefine it in such a way that it is no longer a tug-of-war, then you can win the other side over. In our documentation example, the issue could start out as a "the company is telling us to do more work". This could be redefined as "Other companies have created products that interface with our product. In order for them (and us) to be successful, they have to understand how our product works and so documentation is needed." All of a sudden, what was something that was being created for the faceless company becomes a tool for specific small business owners.

If you can become skilled at learning to distinguish opposition from competition, then you will have a hard-to-find skill that you can start to use proactively. Do a little bit of research on the group that you will be communicating with. If there is strong opposition to what you will be discussing with them, it will probably come out quickly. Look for ways to co-opt or redefine the issue and you'll have accomplished half of your job before you even open your mouth.

Chapter 3

Death To Deadlines! (Ours Not Theirs)

Chapter 3: Death To Deadlines! (Ours Not Theirs)

It is one of life's great truths: deadlines make things happen in negotiations. I'm speaking only for myself, but I suspect that many others would agree that if I can, I'll wait as long as possible before I finally get around to making a decision. Case in point: I've got a high school reunion notice sitting on my desk and I still haven't made up my mind if I'm going to attend. I've got one more week to make up my mind and I'll probably only make my decision on the very last day!

The good thing, sorta, about deadlines is that they create pressure to close. Trust me on this, if it were not for deadlines negotiations could end up taking longer than they already do. The problem with deadlines is that when we are negotiating we tend to be more aware of our time limits rather than those on the other party. Everybody has time limits and we need to be more aware of that. If we focus on just our limits, then this will lead us to under use the strengths that we have and to, unfortunately, overestimate the strength of the other side of the table. Before entering a negotiation, we need to get answers to three deadline related questions:

What Deadlines Are On The Other Party? This is the ultimate question to get an answer to. If you are negotiating to buy a car, the time that the dealership closes will definitely be a deadline for the other party. Get creative and crawl inside the other party's skin and spend some time thinking like they do in order to create a list of their possible deadlines.

What Deadlines Has Your Organization Put On You? This is almost as important as the first question. You need to know what kind of limitations you are dealing with. If you have more time to negotiate then the other side, then great. If not, then you are already in a bind even before the negotiations start.

Is It Possible To Renegotiate The Deadlines That Have Been Put On You? Although not always realized, this is a critical point. Just because you have a deadline, does not mean that you have to live with it. Oftentimes internal deadlines have been created somewhat arbitrarily and can be easily changed. If you can move your deadlines out beyond the other side's deadlines, then you will be in an excellent position even before the negotiations start.

So the key here is to realize that everything in life (including life itself) has a deadline associated with it. As long as you do your research and at least guess at what the other side's deadlines are, then you'll be in good shape to negotiate from a position of strength.

Chapter 4

Real World Negotiating: Boeing vs. The IAM

Chapter 4: Real World Negotiating: Boeing vs. The IAM

If you've been following the news lately, you are probably aware that the International Association of Machinists (IAM) has gone on strike against the Boeing Corporation. News reports are saying that Boeing stands to lose up to $100M every day that the machinists are on strike – wow, that's a lot of money! Boeing's and the IAM's situation provides a unique ecosystem for us to peer into in order to watch a high stakes negotiation while it's in progress. Both sides are actively maneuvering to boost their negotiating power and take power away from the other side so there is a lot for us to learn here.

What's Being Negotiated? The IAM is negotiating a new 3-year contract with Boeing. Note that the contract is fairly short. Boeing likes it this way because they aren't comfortable with their ability to predict the future and they don't want to be required to keep a lot of union workers on staff if the market turns on them in the future.

What's the Hang-Up? The usual key issues revolve around wages and health-care costs. However the big hang up has proved to be job security. Boeing's new 787 Dreamliner program has shown that the company is willing to outsource much of the creation of parts to international suppliers and have local staff just be responsible for final assembly. The current conflict is a direct result of a disagreement over how much say the union should have in future Boeing decisions on how much work should be shipped out to other suppliers.

Why Is This Such A Big Deal? Right now suppliers can deliver parts directly to the Boeing assembly lines. The union workers fear that the next step will be for the suppliers to install their parts directly onto the plane – thus removing the need for the union workers.

What kind of interesting tactics have been used during this negotiation? What's caught my eye is that both sides seem to be trying to influence outside parties in order to apply pressure to the main negotiating parties. Case in point:

Boeing presented a counter proposal to the union just before the Labor Day weekend. It was clear that they were hoping that this proposal would generate a great deal of family dinner table conversation. Boeing was hoping that the machinist's wives/husbands would exert pressure to accept the contact because a strike would become very expensive very quickly in a world with $4/gallon gas.

The IAM's president had met with Boeing's Chairman months ago and warned him that the outsourcing issue would be an important one. Then he told the newspapers that he had told him this.

So what happens now? We'll have to wait and see but it should be quite interesting. Boeing has a backlog of 3,600 planes that are already late for delivery. This strike could cause those planes to slip even more. The union thinks that they have enough leverage that if they have to stay off the job until 2009, they are willing to do so. Let's see who does what next!

Chapter 5

How To Make "Total Cost" Work For You When Negotiating A Sale

Chapter 5: How To Make "Total Cost" Work For You When Negotiating A Sale

I suspect that I'm just about every car salesperson's nightmare. I'm the guy who decides what model car he wants by either personal experience ("I want another one just like that one") or by reading every car review that I can get my hands on. I then go ahead and spend countless hours online and reading the paper comparing prices and availability.

More often than not I'm looking for a used car so issues like mileage, year made, and how many previous owners come into play. Would you want to see me coming in the door of your dealership with my overstuffed folder of backup material?

When I arrive, the single issue that we have to talk about is price. Talk about your win-lose negotiations! Now in all fairness to the car salespeople, they do a good job of trying to expand the discussion from being just about price to a whole host of other items: extended warranty, quality of the repair shop, free oil changes, etc. However, I'm really just interested in talking about the price and I will keep pulling the conversation back to this one basic point over and over again.

Now you might think that this is a fairly poor topic for a blog that purports to be all about "good" negotiating. However, there you would be wrong. For you see my last car purchase went just a bit differently and in that there might be something for all of us to learn.

I had wrecked my previous car and so, unknown to the dealer, I had a serious need to buy. I showed up at the dealer with my paperwork in tow and sat down ready to start my typical price based negotiation. My salesman, Nick, didn't seem to be too phased by my stack of paperwork nor my request to buy his car for $10,000 less than they had it listed for.

Instead, he started off by asking if I had had a chance to shop at any of the other dealers in town. I said that I had. He then asked how that had gone. I told him truthfully that just about everyone seemed to be very nice and that they all had some play in their car prices. He then asked me if all of the cars that I had looked at had a dealer 1-year bumper-to-bumper warrantee? I told him that some did and some didn't.

He nodded and said that all of his cars had this and that it was just proof that the car had been inspected and could be viewed as an insurance policy just in case something happened during the first year. Without actually saying the words, he let me know that there was a value to this warrantee.

Next he asked if I had only looked at cars that had had one owner. I said that I had looked at a mix. He said that when he bought a personal car, he always made sure that it had had a single owner before him – it just kept things simpler he said. Once again, he had implied a value to this feature of the car that I was interested in without actually saying the words.

Finally, he asked if all of the other car dealers had provided me with a CarFax report on the cars that I had looked at. I told him that some did and some didn't. At this point in time he whipped out a CarFax report for the car that I was interested in and asked me to keep it. Once again, Nick was showing the value of how this car dealership did business.

In the end I ended up buying a car from Nick. I was able to get about $3,000 off of their listed price – not the $10,000 that I had originally asked for. However, I still felt that I was getting a good deal. Nick had done a good job of expanding my view of the deal that we were negotiating from being a "price only" deal to including the total cost efficiencies of the deal.

What were the total cost efficiencies for my deal? Well the 1-year bumper-to-bumper warranty had a value of between

$1,200 – $2,000. The one owner feature is a little harder to quantify; however, I'll put it at between $500 – $1000 (to cover hard use repairs). The CarFax report would have cost me about $35.00. Additionally, there was the cost for the time and money that I would have spent driving around to visit more dealerships. In the end, Nick's ability to get me to see the big picture got him the sale and me a car.

Chapter 6

Whatever Happened To That Boeing Negotiation?

Chapter 6: Whatever Happened To That Boeing Negotiation?

We've talked before about the labor negotiations and the strike that is happening at Boeing. Since we last talked, the International Association of Machinists and Aerospace Workers has gone out on strike against Boeing. This has caused Boeing's commercial airplane factories to be idled for over three weeks so far. Probably what's even more important here is that this strike is starting to show signs that it could turn into a protracted standoff. Where's a good negotiator when you need one?

There appear to be two major issues on the table right now: job security and rising health care costs. Both sides seem to feel that if they are the first to suggest a resumption of negotiations, then the other side will believe that they blinked and will negotiate from that position. The end result of all of this is what we've seen in other negotiating situations: the party that hurts the most will be the party that requests to resume negotiations. The strikers will start to feel the pinch from their lost paychecks soon and Boeing is rumored to be losing $100M per day of the strike. Oh, and Boeing has the extra problem that their suppliers are going to start to get skittish when they can't deliver and can't get paid.

Federal negotiators have become involved (that's where the negotiators are!). The union has presented a long list of items that they say must be addressed before they would be willing to accept a new contract. Boeing is trying get the union to shorten the list before they will agree to participate in the negotiations.

Doug Kight is the lead negotiator on the Boeing side. What's interesting is that Doug is the head of HR and has been so for the past two years. Before that he was a lawyer. Hmm, that's all good stuff, but how good of a negotiator do you think he is?

More importantly, has he been involved in major labor negotiations before?

Folks close to the strike believe that it could last 45 days or more. The workers have missed one paycheck so far and the union has started distributing strike pay of $150 / week per member. Meanwhile, suppliers are starting to furlough their workers in order to not create too much of a backlog of parts.

So negotiators what needs to happen here? First, the two sides definitely need to get back together and start talking. It really doesn't matter what they talk about, just start talking. Next, they need to find some common ground. If the union has been able to create a long list of demands, then that's the place to start. Boeing needs to agree to some minor issues and push back on others. This will get the ball rolling. They'll encounter big issues that can't be solved right now, but that's ok – put them off to the side. Eventually all that will be left will be the big issues. Perhaps everyone can agree to go back to work while these are worked on? If not, then both sides need to be willing to give in some. Boeing won't be able to get all of the health costs that they want to push to the workers to be agreed to. However, they can probably get the workers to take up some of the costs. Boeing needs to find ways to keep its workers healthier so that their health costs go down due to lifestyle changes. Boeing can probably get permission to allow some suppliers to get closer to the production line. However, they aren't going to get everything that they are asking for. The workers will have to give a little, but not too much. The real question is just how long it's going to take before both sides can get here…?

Chapter 7

Say Hello To The Bogey-Man – A Negotiator's Best Friend

Chapter 7: Say Hello To The Bogey-Man – A Negotiator's Best Friend

As a negotiator, the key to your long-term success is to have a number of different techniques that you can use when a situation calls for it. One way to think about this is like a carpenter who has a tool belt with his most commonly used tools on it. As the carpenter is working on a job, just about any situation can be solved with one of the tools that he has close at hand. Today we're going to talk about the negotiation equivalent of a carpenter's hammer: a practical, simple, and ethical tool that everyone should know how to use. What's this negotiating tool called you say? The Bogey.

The easiest way to define what the Bogey is, is to show you it in action. Let's say that you want to have your house painted. You have a contractor come out to the house, he looks it over, and then he gives you a quote for $20,000 to do the job. You then tell the contractor "Hey, I love your proposal and I think that you do great work; however, all I have to spend is $17,000 that I got from an insurance claim. Here is a certified check for that amount." The painter accepts your offer and gets to work.

So what happens when you use the Bogey technique? There are three fundamental principles of negotiating that are at work here and it's important that you realize what they are:

 1. By complimenting the painter, you have boosted his ego. He realizes that you now expect something from him in return. In a subtle way, you have actually asked for his help and in most cases you will usually get it.

 2. In all negotiations, the seller knows more about his product than the buyer ever will. The Bogey is one way that the buyer can give the seller a chance to show what they know about the product.

3. One of the fundamental rules of negotiating is that there is always a better deal available for all parties that are participating in the negotiation if only they are willing to search for it. The Bogey technique is how the search for this better deal starts.

When you present a Bogey to a seller, the seller generally won't roll over and accept it. Instead he will come back with a more complete description of what he is selling to you: the quality of his product, his workmanship, the quantity of different items included in his quote, etc. Out of all of this you will now have a much better understanding of what you are buying. Now the real negotiation begins. The seller may lower his price, drop some options, change the delivery schedule, etc. No matter where it goes from here, you will end up ahead of the game.

Chapter 8

Negotiation Awards: Who's The Best Negotiator In The World?

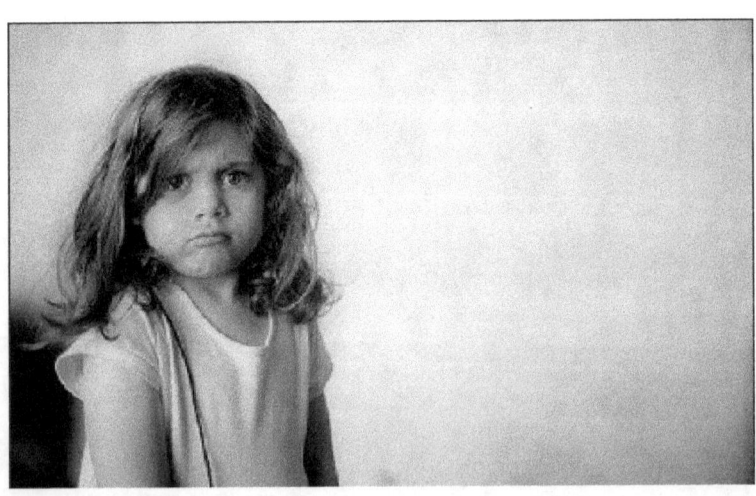

Chapter 8: Negotiation Awards: Who's The Best Negotiator In The World?

We all like to think of ourselves as fairly good negotiators who are constantly getting better. However, it's time that we take a moment and acknowledge that there will always be someone better than us out there. Someone to whom negotiating skills come as almost a second nature. Whose very survival, arguably, could depend on their ability to not only negotiate well but to end up getting their way most of the time. I can almost hear you asking: who is this fantastic manipulator of men and how can I learn from them? Well good news, you've probably already met them: professional negotiators will almost all agree that the best negotiators in the world are two-year-olds.

Why two-year-olds you ask? Well take just a moment and think about it. If a two-year-old makes a request and then does not get his/her way, what will they do? They'll fall to the floor and start to cry, scream, kick their feet and maybe even hold their breath until they get their way.

If you've ever been the target of one of these fits, you know just how powerfully effective they can be. You just want the kid to stop! This is where the negotiating starts. If the parent tries to appease the child by begging, pleading, or even offering them bribes to stop their behavior then the child will have learned an important lesson: throwing a fit works. This means that the next time that the child wants something, he/she will have the fit as one of their known successful negotiating techniques.

If, however, the parent is strong enough to just walk away and let the child wear themselves out with no effect, then once again the child will have learned something: a fit does not work. In this case the parent's negotiating technique has taught the child something and so the child will adjust their technique next time: they'll try something else. The next time that the child wants something, perhaps they will hug their parent or say that they love them or something else along those lines in order to see if this achieves a better result.

We can all learn something each time we negotiate and a two-year-old has a great deal to teach us. A child's ability to try new negotiating techniques, retain those that work and discard those that don't work, should be showing us the way that we need to be constantly refining our techniques. All too often I encounter people who view negotiating as a "process" to be learned and repeated over and over again in every situation. This couldn't be further from the truth.

A better way of thinking about negotiating is to view it as a specialized form of communication. When we negotiate we are trying to get something that we want by interacting with someone else who is trying to do the exact same thing. Every negotiation is different and every individual that we negotiate with is different. This means that there IS NO FIXED FORMULA for negotiating. Rather, skilled negotiators have a collection of skills that they can use as they see fit to do so. I guess the best analogy would be to a carpenter. Every piece of wood is different and depending on what the carpenter wants to create out of the wood, he will choose to use any one of a large collection of specialized tools that he has to work with.

Years ago I used to watch the This Old House TV show in which Norm Abrams would do fantastic things with wood as part of a house remodeling job. It took me a long time to realize that not only was Norm a gifted craftsman, but he also had every specialty wood working tool known to man. He would smoothly swap out tools as he transformed a tree stump into a fantastic Adirondack chair. If Norm was a negotiator, we'd be seeing him swap negotiating skills in and out as he searched for the right tools needed to turn a negotiation into a success.

If you've been looking for the one negotiating "system" that will allow you to "win" all of your negotiations, it's time to give it up. Such a system does not exist and any two-year-old can tell you this. However, if you can understand that like a master carpenter, you can collect the right negotiating tools and by choosing the right tools for the right situation, you can create negotiation results that are things of beauty.

Chapter 9

It's Negotiation Time At Boeing: Plane & Simple

Chapter 9: It's Negotiation Time At Boeing: Plane & Simple

Even as the rest of the world is going through a financial meltdown, out in Seattle there is still strike going on at Boeing that is costing the company roughly $100M in missed revenue per day. Ouch! Just in case you have not been following this story, the 27,000 members of the International Associaition of Machinists and Aerospace Workers who work for Boeing are out on strike and have been so for since September 6th. Doesn't this seem like just the kind of problem that a good negotiator could step in and solve?

Currently, both sides are feeling the pain from the strike. On this past Wednesday Boeing had to announce to the press that their 3rd quarter net income sank by 38% due to the strike. Now you've got to remember that Boeing is sitting on a stack of orders for their planes right now: they have a backlog of orders for 3,725 planes of which about 900 are for the eagerly anticipated new 787 Dreamliner. Keep in mind that a new airplane costs roughly about $100M to buy and you start to understand that if only Boeing could build new airplanes, then they would be making money hand over fist.

The union folks are also hurting. On average the union workers bring home about $65,000 / year. While the strike is on, they are getting $150 / week from the union in strike pay. This means that everyone is scrambling to pick up part-time jobs in order to stem the bleeding.

The main players in this negotiating drama are well known. On the union side they have Mark Blondin who is a former Boeing machinist who is serving as the lead negotiator for the union. On Boeing's side, Doug Kight who is Boeing's lead negotiator. Kight is also Boeing's vice president of human resources, a position that he took over in late 2006. During previous negotiations, Kight provided legal counsel to his predecessor, Jerry Calhoun, who was formerly Boeing's lead negotiator.

When we talk about negotiating deals, we often focus on price. However, in this case the price issue is well hidden by another issue: job security. At the heart of the debate is a single question: can Boeing expand the types of jobs that outside contractors perform in assembling airplanes. From Boeing's point-of-view they are trying to cut costs and reduce the time required to build a plane. In order to do this they are outsourcing jobs to other firms. As a result of the last contract that was negotiated between these two parties, outside firms are now allowed to deliver parts directly to the assembly line. The union is concerned that their members are going to lose their jobs to outside firms if this trend continues. Boeing says that they need to retain flexibility and are unwilling to make any job guarantees. Can you say deadlock?

What can be done to resolve this issue? Remember, the ultimate goal is to make sure that both sides of the table leave the negotiations with a feeling of satisfaction. Additionally, both sides need to give something up in order to feel that they've "earned" a negotiated settlement. There are lots of ways that this issue can be resolved. Here's one that would work for both sides.

I'm sure that there are a lot of other issues on the table like health care, pension benefits, etc. Let's assume that the core negotiating concept of expanding the discussion has been done and that this issue of job security is really, really a key sticking point. If you focus for a moment on the end game, Boeing really wants to start making planes again so that they can keep their customers and make lots of money. The union members really want to start making planes again because they miss their paychecks and they are proud of their work. This is great news – both sides want the same final goal. Now the trick is to see what can be done in order to get them there.

One thing that makes solving this issue just a bit easier is that Boeing is sitting on a pile of money. Boeing has two issues with the union: the immediate issue of job security for 27,000 workers as well as the long term life of the union itself (will a union be needed in the future?). Both needs have to be met. The union has two issues with Boeing: Boeing wants to lower it's production costs by using less expensive outsourced labor and Boeing is getting tired of having to deal with a strike and work stoppage every three years. The strikes are playing havoc with Boeing's ability to compete with Airbus because Boeing can't honor its contracts to its customers.

So here's one possible solution. Boeing has 27,000 current employees who basically (just like all of us) only really care about their jobs. What Boeing should agree to is that they will keep these employees working until such time as they no longer need them. At that point in time, Boeing will pay them off to go away. Specifically, Boeing will pay them 1/2 their current salary though retirement age. This will free the worker up to go get retrained and get another job if they want to. Potentially they could earn a great deal of money for the rest of their career. Oh, and they could pretty much pick any job that would make them happy because they would still be getting paid by Boeing. This would cost Boeing some serious cash. If they terminated all 27,000 workers who were making $65,000 / year and everyone was 30 years old, then Boeing would have to pay out $30B over the next 35 years. Now that sounds like a lot of money, but it turns out that it really isn't. Remember we're really talking about a long-term solution here. Boeing is going to be paying a lot in salary no matter what. Having the flexibility to further streamline their production process while potentially paying half of that would save the company a lot of money.

Now from the union's position, they are going to have to change how they operate in the future. Clearly the number of machinists needed by Boeing has been and will continue to decrease over time. However, it can be argued that the remaining machinists will become even more important to the company – they will be doing things that no outsourcing firm can do. The role of the union is going to have to evolve and change. Specifically, over time the machinist union will need to merge with another union in order to maintain it's bargaining strength. Realizing this earlier than later will be the key to resolving the current issues.

Chapter 10

Top 10 Secrets To Make A Negotiation Work Out For You!

Chapter 10: Top 10 Secrets To Make A Negotiation Work Out For You!

Often times the thought of having to negotiate with someone for something can be quite intimidating. I mean, we live in the world of Amazon's one-click purchasing, no haggle car buying, and we visit the home of low-low prices, we don't HAVE to negotiate for most of the things that we want. However, if you take just a moment to think about it, when it comes down to the things that we REALLY, REALLY want in this life, we almost always seem to end up negotiating for them. Case in point: a house, a nice car, your next job, etc. If it's valuable, then it sure seems like some sort of negotiation is called for.

All this being said, if negotiating is so important to getting what we want, then why do we get so nervous when we are facing a negotiating situation? It's my belief that one of the key reasons that nobody seems to really look forward to to a negotiation is because we don't believe that we know how to negotiate. With so many other things in life, there are some basic rules, some things to practice, and then poof – you can determine how good you are at doing it. Things that fall into this category are playing tennis, running a marathon, playing golf, baking a cake, etc. Negotiating is not nearly so nice & neat.

The challenge to becoming a good negotiator is to first realize that there is no magic "silver bullet" skill that you need to learn in order to become an accomplished negotiator. Instead, there are a whole bunch of "little" skills that when put together can make you a negotiating force. In order to help you get started on your path to becoming the negotiator that you always wanted to be, here are 10 secrets that all the great negotiators use:

1. Remember that a negotiation is NOT a contest. There is not a winner & a loser, rather a better deal can always be found for both parties.

2. Surprisingly enough, you really do have more power than you may think that you do. Be sure to always be looking for ways in which the other side of the table's power may be more limited than you originally thought.

3. Always write down your negotiating plan BEFORE you start to negotiate. Make sure that during the negotiations you never decide an issue unless you have had a chance to prepare for it. Make sure that you follow your negotiating plan that you made before you started.

4. Don't be afraid to negotiate no matter how much you might think that the other side has an overwhelming position. Just remember – they might be feeling exactly the same way!

5. Get the best – don't enter into a negotiation with an inferior team.

6. Get your shots before you negotiate! Make sure that you (and your team) have prepared your immune system to defend your positions before you start to negotiate.

7. Talk less – listen more. Oh, and don't be critical when you are listening.

8. Ignore title – don't let the other side of the table intimidate you with their titles or status. Do your homework and then be willing to confront them.

9. Facts can be bent. Make sure that you are not intimidated by facts, averages, or even statistics that are presented by the other side of the table.

10. If a deadlock occurs, don't spend time talking about all of your problems – the other side has their own and it's not helpful to spend time talking about yours.

Chapter 11

Negotiation Firestarter: The Take It Or Leave It Tactic

Chapter 11: Negotiation Firestarter: The Take It Or Leave It Tactic

If you really want to set off the other side of the table during a negotiation, one great way to do this is to tell them that they can "take it or leave it." This is pretty much the verbal equivalent of throwing gas on a fire – you are guaranteed to generate hostility on the other side of the table when you use this phrase.

We react in exactly the same way if the other side tries this tactic on us during a negotiation. This is understandable; however, if we take just a moment to think about it, we should probably be used to dealing with this negotiating tactic.

The deals that are presented to you in the course of an average day are almost all of the "take it or leave" it nature. You see these types of deals in the insurance bills that you get, the groceries that you buy, and the parking ticket that you pay. Although they might not say it explicitly, these are all subtle forms of the "take it or leave it" tactic.

Before you decide to burst into flames the next time that someone uses this tactic on you, take a moment and give some thought to why the other side might be using this tactic. They have decided to only offer a fixed price and here are some of the reasons that they might be doing this:

1. They don't want every one of their employees to have to have good negotiating skills or to take the time that a negotiation requires in order to successfully complete a deal.

2. They might be willing to negotiate with you on this deal; however, they don't want to have to negotiate with you in the future.

3. If they negotiated with you and ended up lowering their price, then they would have to lower their price for all of their customers.

4. They know that you cannot afford to "leave it".

5. They have already dealt with many other customers who had no problem paying their fixed price.

6. They can't afford to lower their price anymore because they are already selling at their rock bottom price.

When you look at it this way, you'll realize that most business is normally done using the "take it or leave it" tactic no matter what we choose to call it. We need to realize that many prices are set because of existing laws or regulations.

If you find yourself in the position of having to use the "take it or leave it" tactic during a negotiation, then you need to search for ways to reduce the natural hostility that this is going to cause in the other side.

Here are the best methods for reducing hostility when you decide to offer only a "fixed price" to the other side:

1. Show the laws / regulations that are causing you to have to offer the product at the stated price.

2. Show the company policy that requires the product to be offered at the given price.

3. Publish a price list.

4. Publish a standard list of discounts.

5. Display the price of your product / service where everyone can see it.

6. Provide proof that shows all potential customers that the price that you are using is the same price that is being offered to everyone.

7. Simply make sure that you provide a good justification for the price that you are using.

As always in any negotiation situation, the more discussions that can be held face-to-face the better the negotiations will go. Listen to what the other side has to say and make sure that everyone has a chance to save face and come out ahead.

Chapter 12

Negotiating Self Defense: Countering The Reverse Auction Tactic

Chapter 12: Negotiating Self Defense: Countering The Reverse Auction Tactic

I've always liked superheros. From my earliest days of reading comic books to my current-day trips to the movie theater to see Spiderman and Iron Man, I just don't seem to be able to get my fill of superheros.

I believe that superheros, although fictional (probably – however I still have hope), can teach us a lot about how to become better negotiators. One lesson that all superheros seem to learn in superhero school is that in order to be successful in a fight, they always need to have good self defense skills.

In negotiations, sellers need to have a good defense against one negotiating tactic that a buyer can use which is called the "reverse auction". It works like this: let's pretend that you wanted to build buy a new car. You visit three different car dealers and get three different offers. As you can imagine, each of these offers will contain a confusing mix of different financing and option packages.

Your next step will be to call a "reverse auction". You go back to each dealer and tell them that you've visited the other two dealers. Each dealer will then proceed to tell you why they are the best and why you should avoid buying from the other dealers. After you've had a chance to talk with all three dealers, you now understand the subtleties and the options associated with buying the car that you want.

With all of this new information, you are now able to more clearly refine your specifications because the alternatives have become clear. You can now specify the specific financing and option packages that the dealers can bid on.

You will end up selecting the dealer who can provide the best price while providing the most car for that price. By using a reverse auction, the buyer was able to learn a great deal about buying a specific new car and was able to trade off options that he/she originally did not know existed.

All of this is great if you are a buyer, but what if you are the seller (or the dealer in the case of our example)?

It turns out that although it may initially appear as though the buyer is holding all the cards when they are using the reverse auction tactic, that's not really true – you still have a great deal of negotiating power.

Check out my reverse auction training video here by clicking here!

Your greatest strength comes from the simple fact that the reverse auction takes a great deal of the buyer's time in order to do correctly. They have to identify sellers, collect bids, evaluate, revisit to collect information, and then revisit again to negotiate a final deal. All this takes time that they may not have to give.

What you need to do is to present yourself as being the seller who best understands that the buyer's needs are. If you can convince him of your credibility then you'll be well positioned to close the deal.

Here are a few tips that will help you come out ahead when your buyer decides to us the reverse auction tactic on you:

1. **Be Last**: You want to be the last person that the buyer talks with, not the first. This may allow you to short-circuit the reverse auction process.

2. **Use Your Best**: When dealing with the buyer, you want to use either your best negotiators or at least make sure that you are well prepared for the discussion (no distractions!).

3. **Give In Slowly**: This is always a good tip – do not hurry to make concessions to the buyer.

4. **Sell, Sell, Sell**: Make sure that you sell the buyer on your strengths and benefits.

5. **Use Limits**: Clearly communicate to the buyer that the scope of your authority is limited in this deal to the bottom-line figure.

6. **Use Experts**: The buyer is desperately looking for somebody to believe in so that they can be convinced that you are the right one to buy from. Make sure that you provide the expert that they need to find.

7. **Use Innovation As A Back-Up**: Life is unpredictable. Sometimes a reverse auction will start to go badly for you. In these cases, you need to make sure that you have a new and innovative approach that you can whip out if this happens – lifetime free oil changes anyone?

8. **Find The Decision Maker**: You can talk with the buyer until you are blue in the face, but it will be all for naught if you haven't done your homework and made sure that they really are the final decision maker. Check before you invest the time and energy.

It's from the forge of failure that the steel of success is formed.

Hard Work Does Not Guarantee Success, But Success Does Not Happen Without Hard Work.

- Dr. Jim Anderson

Create An Effective Negotiating Team At Your Company!

Dr. Jim Anderson is available to provide training and coaching on the topics that are the most important to people who have to negotiate: how can my team effectively prepare for and execute a successful negotiation that will get us what we both want and need?

Dr. Anderson believes that in order to both learn and remember what he says, audiences need to laugh. Each one of his speeches is full of fun and humor so that what he says "sticks" with everyone.

Dr. Anderson's Negotiating Training Includes:

1. How to plan for a negotiation: what information do you need and where can you find it?

2. What's the best way to explore how a deal can be created during a negotiation?

3. How can you bring a negotiation to a close without giving in to the other side?

Dr. Jim Anderson works with over 100 customers per year. To invite Dr. Anderson to work with you, contact him at:

Phone: 813-418-6970 or
Email: jim@BlueElephantConsulting.com

Photo Credits:

Cover - Brian Bennett

https://www.flickr.com/photos/umpqua/

Chapter 1 - Roberta R.

https://www.flickr.com/photos/wererabbit/

Chapter 2 – TELETOONlanuit

https://www.flickr.com/photos/46914336@N05/

Chapter 3 – openDemocracy

https://www.flickr.com/photos/opendemocracy/

Chapter 4 - Andrea Giardina

https://www.flickr.com/photos/ilgattodelvicino/

Chapter 5 - Christopher Allison Photography

https://www.flickr.com/photos/caharley72/

Chapter 6 - Global Panorama

https://www.flickr.com/photos/121483302@N02/

Chapter 7 - Jim Purbrick

https://www.flickr.com/photos/jimpurbrick/

Chapter 8 - greg westfall

https://www.flickr.com/photos/imagesbywestfall/

Chapter 9 - Andrew W. Sieber

https://www.flickr.com/photos/smartjunco/

Chapter 10 - Sam Churchill

https://www.flickr.com/photos/samchurchill/

Chapter 11 – Amazon

https://www.amazon.com/Todays-Vintage-Locker-Refrigerator-Magnet/dp/B004ICJMW8

Chapter 12 - Ape Lad

https://www.flickr.com/photos/apelad/

Other Books By The Author

Product Management

- How Product Managers Can Sell More Of Their Product: Tips & Techniques For Product Managers To Better Understand How To Sell Their Product

- How Product Managers Can Sell More Of Their Product: Tips & Techniques For Product Managers To Better Understand How To Sell Their Product

- How To Create A Successful Product That Customers Will Want: Techniques For Product Managers To Boost Product Sales And Increase Customer Satisfaction

- What Product Managers Need To Know About World-Class Product Development: How Product Managers Can Create Successful Products

- How Product Managers Can Learn To Understand Their Customers: Techniques For Product Managers To Better Understand What Their Customers Really Want

- Product Management Secrets: Techniques For Product Managers To Boost Produ Michael Kct Sales And Increase Customer Satisfaction

- Product Development Lessons For Product Managers: How Product Managers Can Create Successful Products

- Customer Lessons For Product Managers: Techniques For Product Managers To Better Understand What Their Customers Really Want

- Product Failure Lessons For Product Managers: Examples Of Products That Have Failed For Product Managers To Learn From

- Communication Skills For Product Managers: The Communication Skills That Product Managers Need To Know How To Use In Order To Have A Successful Product

- How To Have A Successful Product Manager Career: The Things That You Need To Be Doing TODAY In Order To Have A Successful Product Manager Career

- Product Manager Product Success: How to keep your product on track and make it become a success

Public Speaking

- How To Organize A Speech In Order To Make Your Point: How to put together a speech that will capture and hold your audience's attention

- Changing How You Speak To Overcome Your Fear Of Speaking: Change techniques that will transform a speech into a memorable event

- Delivering Excellence: How To Give Presentations That Make A Difference: Presentation techniques that will transform a speech into a memorable event

- Tools Speakers Need In Order To Give The Perfect Speech: What tools to use to create your next speech so that your message will be remembered forever!

- How To Create A Speech That Will Be Remembered

- Secrets To Organizing A Speech For Maximum Impact: How to put together a speech that will capture and hold your audience's attention

- How To Become A Better Speaker By Changing How You Speak: Change techniques that will transform a speech into a memorable event

- How To Give A Great Presentation: Presentation techniques that will transform a speech into a memorable event

- How To Rehearse In Order To Give The Perfect Speech: How to effectively rehearse your next speech to that your message be remembered forever!

- Secrets To Creating The Perfect Speech: How to create a speech that will make your message be remembered forever!

- Secrets To Organizing The Perfect Speech: How to organize the best speech of your life!

- Secrets To Planning The Perfect Speech: How to plan to give the best speech of your life

- How To Show What You Mean During A Presentation: How to use visual techniques to transform a speech into a memorable event

CIO Skills

- New IT Technology Issues Facing CIOs: How CIOs Can Stay On Top Of The Changes In The Technology That Powers The Company

- Keeping The Barbarians Out: How CIOs Can Secure Their Department and Company: Tips And Techniques For CIOs To Use In Order To Secure Both Their IT Department And Their Company

- What CIOs Need To Know In Order To Successfully Manage An IT Department: Decision Making Skills That Every CIO Needs To Have In Order To Be Able To Make The Right Choices

- Becoming A Powerful And Effective Leader: Tips And Techniques That IT Managers Can Use In Order To Develop Leadership Skills

- CIO Secrets For Growing Innovation: Tips And Techniques For CIOs To Use In Order To Make Innovation Happen In Their IT Department

- Your Success As A CIO Depends On How Well You Communicate: Tips And Techniques For CIOs To Use In Order To Become Better Communicators

- What CIOs Need To Know About Working With Partners: Techniques For CIOs To Use In Order To Be Able To Successfully Work With Partners

- Critical CIO Management Skills: Decision Making Skills That Every CIO Needs To Have In Order To Be Able To Make The Right Choices

- How CIOs Can Make Innovation Happen: Tips And Techniques For CIOs To Use In Order To Make Innovation Happen In Their IT Department

- CIO Communication Skills Secrets: Tips And Techniques For CIOs To Use In Order To Become Better Communicators

- Managing Your CIO Career: Steps That CIOs Have To Take In Order To Have A Long And Successful Career

- CIO Business Skills: How CIOs can work effectively with the rest of the company!

IT Manager Skills

- How IT Managers Can Use New Technology To Meet Today's IT Challenges: Technologies That IT Managers Can Use In Order to Make Their Teams More Productive

- How To Build High Performance IT Teams: Tips And Techniques That IT Managers Can Use In Order To Develop Productive Teams

- Save Yourself, Save Your Job – How To Manage Your IT Career: Secrets That IT Managers Can Use

In Order To Have A Successful Career

- Growing Your CIO Career: How CIOs Can Work With The Entire Company In Order To Be Successful

- How IT Managers Can Make Innovation Happen: Tips And Techniques For IT Managers To Use In Order To Make Innovation Happen In Their Teams

- Staffing Skills IT Managers Must Have: Tips And Techniques That IT Managers Can Use In Order To Correctly Staff Their Teams

- Secrets Of Effective Leadership For IT Managers: Tips And Techniques That IT Managers Can Use In Order To Develop Leadership Skills

- IT Manager Career Secrets: Tips And Techniques That IT Managers Can Use In Order To Have A Successful Career

- IT Manager Budgeting Skills: How IT Managers Can Request, Manage, Use, And Track Their Funding

- Secrets Of Managing Budgets: What IT Managers Need To Know In Order To Understand How Their Company Uses Money

Negotiating

- Exploring How To Get The Deal That You Want In A Negotiation: How To Develop The Skill Of Exploring What Is Possible In A Negotiation In Order To Reach The Best Possible Deal

- Use The Power Of Arguing To Win Your Next Negotiation: How To Develop The Skill Of Effective Arguing In A Negotiation In Order To Get The Best Possible Outcome

- Learn How To Signal In Your Next Negotiation: How To Develop The Skill Of Effective Signaling In A Negotiation In Order To Get The Best Possible Outcome

- Learn The Skill Of Exploring In A Negotiation: How To Develop The Skill Of Exploring What Is Possible In A Negotiation In Order To Reach The Best Possible Deal

- Learn How To Argue In Your Next Negotiation: How To Develop The Skill Of Effective Arguing In A Negotiation In Order To Get The Best Possible Outcome|

- How To Open Your Next Negotiation: How To Start A Negotiation In Order To Get The Best Possible

Outcome

- Preparing For Your Next Negotiation: What You Need To Do BEFORE A Negotiation Starts In Order To Get The Best Possible Deal

- Learn How To Package Trades In Your Next Negotiation

- All Good Things Come To An End: How To Close A Negotiation - How To Develop The Skill Of Closing In Order To Get The Best Possible Outcome From A Negotiation

- Take No Prisoners In Your Next Negotiation: How To Start A Negotiation In Order To Get The Best Possible Outcome

Miscellaneous

- How To Heal A Broken Leg – Fast!: Understanding how to deal with a broken leg in order to start walking again quickly

- How Software Defined Networking (SDN) Is Going To Change Your World Forever: The Revolution In Network Design And How It Affects You

- The Power Of Virtualization: How It Affects Memory, Servers, and Storage: The Revolution In Creating Virtual Devices And How It Affects You

- The Internet-Enabled Successful School District Superintendent: How To Use The Internet To Boost Parental Involvement In Your Schools

- Power Distribution Unit (PDU) Secrets: What Everyone Who Works In A Data Center Needs To Know!

- Making The Jump: How To Land Your Dream Job When You Get Out Of College!

- How To Use The Internet To Create Successful Students And Involved Parents

How To Develop The Skill Of Effective Signaling In A Negotiation In Order To Get The Best Possible Outcome

This book has been written with one goal in mind – to show you how to successfully signal in your next negotiation. It's not easy being a negotiator and so we're going to show you how to successfully communicate to the other side what you really want them to do.

Let's Make Your Negotiation A Success!

What You'll Find Inside:

- **DEMANDS & DEADLINES: YOUR TWO BEST FRIENDS**

- **SAY HELLO TO THE BOGEY-MAN – A NEGOTIATOR'S BEST FRIEND**

- **NEGOTIATION FIRESTARTER: THE TAKE IT OR LEAVE IT TACTIC**

- **NEGOTIATING SELF DEFENSE: COUNTERING THE REVERSE AUCTION TACTIC**

Dr. Jim Anderson brings his 25 years of real-world experience to this book. He's been a negotiator at some of the world's largest firms. He's going to show you what you need to do (and not do!) in order to get the best deal out of your next negotiation!

www.ingramcontent.com/pod-product-compliance
Lightning Source LLC
Chambersburg PA
CBHW061203180526
45170CB00002B/939